JIM BRANDENBURG

An American Safari

ADVENTURES ON THE
NORTH AMERICAN PRAIRIE

Edited by JOANN BREN GUERNSEY

WALKER AND COMPANY ❋ NEW YORK

First published in the United States of America in 1995
by Walker Publishing Company, Inc.

Published simultaneously in Canada by Thomas Allen
& Son Canada, Limited, Markham, Ontario

Library of Congress Cataloging-in-Publication Data
Brandenburg, Jim.
    An American safari : adventures on the North American prairie /
Jim Brandenburg ; edited by JoAnn Bren Guernsey.
        p.   cm.
    Includes index.
    ISBN 0-8027-8319-8 (hc). — ISBN 0-8027-8320-1 (reinf)
    1. Prairie ecology—United States—Juvenile literature.
2. Prairie fauna—United States—Juvenile literature. [1. Prairie
ecology. 2. Ecology. 3. Prairie animals.] I. Guernsey, JoAnn
Bren. II. Title.
QH104.B73   1995
508.73'09145—dc20   94-24654
                                                      CIP
                                                      AC

Book design by Victoria Hartman

Printed in Hong Kong

10 9 8 7 6 5 4 3 2 1

☙ ☙ ☙ *Contents*

Chapter 1

BIRTH OF A DREAM

I grew up in southern Minnesota, not far from the South Dakota border. Even though I was surrounded by cornfields and overgrazed pasture, I always seemed to be aware of this land as it used to be—a prairie displaying its rich tapestry of grasses and wildflowers. I envisioned the vibrant reds and purples and golds stretching all the way to the horizon, set into motion by a breeze or fleeting cloud shadow. In my imagination, buffalo herds raised smoky dust, and the earth rumbled beneath their hooves.

Only a few pieces of this endangered system remained near my home, mostly in ditches, along railroad tracks, and at the edges of graveyards. In one area, however, natural prairie had survived in a slightly larger piece. The Blue Mounds—a big uplifting of the earth that was so full of rocks, a plow couldn't break through it—offered me the chance to walk away from my landscape of silos and barns and machinery and people to find something better: animals. My relationship with wildlife took time to evolve into what it is now, however. For I was a hunter when I was a boy.

I would search for tracks and wonder about them—what creature had made the tracks, where had it slept, what had it eaten? And then I would shoot the rabbits or squirrels or whatever and carry home the carcasses as trophies.

Facing page: A herd of bison emerge from the mist on Houck Ranch, South Dakota.

Early one morning, I stumbled across a young red fox in a pasture about two miles from my home. I can still see that startled fox on a hill across from me, cutting through the dewy grass with its bright red plume of a tail. From that day on, I became a fox fanatic. I tracked them for miles and hours through new snow, my toes and fingers growing numb but the rest of me warmed by the possibility of that flash of red fur just ahead. I studied foxes. And, yes, I also hunted and trapped them.

Until one day when I found a small plastic Argus camera on a card table in the drugstore. It was on sale for three dollars. Not long afterward, I again found myself face-to-face with a red fox. But that day something led me to hunt with my new camera instead of my usual traps and gun.

Above: An island of virgin prairie in a suburb of Chicago.

Left: A cottontail rabbit appears to be yawning near a prairie dog burrow in western South Dakota.

Facing page: A remnant patch of cord grass persists in the midst of a plowed field.

My first wildlife photograph brought me face-to-face with a young red fox.

The fox was off in the distance. Since I had discovered that you can call in a fox by sounding like a mouse, I hid behind a big rock and squeaked. The young animal was so programmed to hunt that squeaky mouse, he couldn't quite connect the sound with a human. He came right up to me!

During those brief moments of his confusion, I stood there and clicked away with my new camera. Eight pictures of one subject from one spot. This is probably the first evidence of my future as a professional photographer since most people, especially kids, just snap a picture and figure, "there—got it."

When I had the film developed that day, I discovered something. That camera was magic. Rather than bringing home a "trophy" that was really only an animal's dead, furry body . . . gone forever, now I could bring home something more magical: a *moment*. A moment I can still look at today. Whenever I do, I am transported to that prairie scene—the silence, the fragrant breeze, the thrilling, unexpected exchange between two very different creatures.

It's been more than thirty years since I last pursued any animal with a gun instead of a camera. But those early hunting trips on the prairie laid the groundwork for my future as a wildlife photographer and environmental activist. Though my work has taken me all over the world, I still feel the pull of home—the urge to explore what is left of the American prairie and to play a role in its restoration before it's too late.

ꙮ ꙮ ꙮ *Chapter 2*

A LANDSCAPE NEARLY LOST

Monarch butterflies rest on blazing star in the cool morning air.

Less than two centuries ago, nearly a quarter of North America was covered with grass. Not the kind of grass you mow in front of your house but a living carpet splashed with color and texture. Although grasses dominated, many of the plants found in the prairie were wildflowers. And, of course, all those blossoms drew an abundance of butterflies and other insects, all adding to the brilliance and buzz of the region.

Above: Purple coneflower — one of the many medicinal plants of the prairie.

Left: A female redwing blackbird pauses as it brings food to its nearby nestling.

Bison at Wind Cave National Park after a roll in the dirt, which is called wallowing.

Beneath the surface of the prairie, for thousands of square miles, black-tailed prairie dogs had dug elaborate "towns," which supported them along with an astonishing variety of other animals. Grazing on this prairie were about sixty to seventy million bison (often called buffalo), fifty million pronghorn (American antelope), and countless elk and deer.

Before the midsection of North America was turned into cropland and cattle ranches in the mid-1800s to feed its human inhabitants, it was divided into three distinct belts of prairie: shortgrass, mixed-grass, and tallgrass. Just east of the Rockies and bordering the desert terrain was the shortgrass prairie. Less than twelve inches tall, these grasses needed almost no rain to survive. In the middle of the continent, between the other two belts, was an area known as the mixed-grass prairie because it combined elements of both.

Above: The American elk, or wapiti, was originally a prairie animal.

Left: An alert prairie dog scrutinizes an unconcerned buck antelope.

Prairie lands in the United States. (Present prairie data provided by U.S.G.S. Eros Data Center and Manitoba Centre for Remote Sensing, used by permission of National Geographic Society Cartographic Division.)

The prairie belt farthest east was named for its tall grasses. A yearly average of thirty inches of rain fueled growth of half an inch or more each day and resulted in grasses reaching up to twelve feet high. Of the three prairie types, the tallgrass is sometimes called the true prairie system, parts of which have been found to host 200–400 species of plants. The tallgrass prairie is also the most endangered. Less than .01 percent remains of the original 140 million acres of rich, organic tallgrass prairie.

Prairies were essentially treeless areas. Vegetation growth was controlled by rainfall and by frequent fire. Prairie fires—powerful

The tallgrass prairie burned frequently, sometimes at the hands of Native Americans and sometimes by lightning. This is a controlled burn to restore the prairie at The Nature Conservancy's Tallgrass Prairie Preserve in Oklahoma.

displays called "Red Buffalo" by Plains Indians because the roar of the flames sounded like a thundering herd—were usually sparked by lightning. But people also set fires intentionally to clear dead vegetation and encourage more rapid growth of the deep-rooted grasses. Without controlled burning, mixed and tall grasses struggle to survive—along with the animals that depend on them—and trees take over.

Many of the earth's natural habitats have been used and abused by humans, but perhaps none more than the grasslands. The richness of the soil made it productive farmland, and the broad flatness of it was perfect for raising cattle. The North American prairie was an irresistible place for our pioneer ancestors to claim as their own . . . and to change.

Above: Sunrise and the king of the tallgrass prairie—big bluestem.

Facing page: A bison herd rests peacefully in the shadow of the Black Hills, an area sacred to the Sioux. Smoke from a forest fire is seen in the background.

Prairie dogs spend hour after hour grooming. Using their long, curved front teeth as a comb, they remove dirt and parasites from one another's fur. This habit appears to be as much for the sake of socializing as it is for cleanliness.

Facing page, top: The ferruginous hawk, also called prairie eagle by the pioneers because of its large size.

Facing page, bottom: Prairie dog giving its warning bark in the midst of a herd of bison.

🐾 🐾 🐾 *Chapter 3*

LITTLE TOWN ON THE PRAIRIE

In 1974 I learned that Time-Life Books was publishing a series called The American Wilderness, and I longed to be a part of it. But when I called up Time-Life in New York, I wasn't surprised by rejection. I was, after all, just a struggling journalist in his twenties working for a small-town newspaper in Minnesota.

I had to try to prove myself, so, with the knowledge that Time-Life's next book was about the Northwest coast, I took three weeks off from work and headed west. Paying all my own expenses and without any guarantee that I'd sell a single photo, I shot every waking minute of every day. What an honor it was when Time-Life chose two of my photos!

This led to my first assignment for a national publication—the Time-Life book about the Badlands of South Dakota. The subject for my chapter of this book was one of the most fascinating, complex ecosystems in the world: the bustling "town" of the black-tailed prairie dog.

These plump, rabbit-size rodents live underground, where they escape from predators and withstand bitter winters, sizzling summers, floods, and fires. Probably the most social rodents in existence, prairie dogs have developed a social system based on the fact that 1,000 pairs of watchful eyes are better than one.

When sensing danger, perhaps a golden eagle circling above, a prairie dog takes the time before seeking shelter for itself to sound an alarm to its neighbors. It jumps or stretches tall on hind legs, flinging its front legs and nose skyward, and barks (the prairie dog was named for the barking sounds it makes). While warning the others, it may begin to ease one foot into its burrow. Within seconds, the whole town disappears underground.

Prairie dog pups practice their warning barks in the afternoon sun.

I recall the first time I watched several pups learning to bark, all lined up like little soldiers alongside their mother. Their practice barks were more like hiccups, and their attempted leaps often resulted in them toppling over backward. But they kept trying, and other adults emerged from underground to stand tall and alert. I was looking at them through my lens, their scattered outlines glowing against a sunset. Like candles on a birthday cake.

Prairie dogs bark in response to many different situations, sometimes even at butterflies. Because of all this vocalizing, the town might be in constant panic if it weren't for the fact that the barking sounds form a language. Different signals mean different prey, levels of danger, or "all clear," and everyone seems to know how to react. The danger-in-the-sky warning bark is the most urgent of all.

A prairie dog town is divided into neighborhoods; dozens of animals appear to know each other, communicate with each other, help each other build their homes, and even occasionally feed each other's young. They share sentry duty, and it is common to see four

Above: A prairie dog's diet consists primarily of grasses, roots, and seeds, although they sometimes eat insects. They prefer to sit upright and keep alert while they eat. Gnawing on plants not only fills their stomachs but also keeps the grasses surrounding their burrows short enough so they can always have a clear view.

Left: A pair of prairie dogs "kiss" and groom each other.

prairie dogs standing guard at once, each facing a different direction for as long as a half hour.

Inside a prairie dog burrow are one or more long tunnels a few feet below the ground. Several rooms lie along each tunnel. Those nearest the entrance are usually used as listening posts and turn-around ledges. Other chambers include food storage rooms, toilets, and nurseries where the young lie in nests of dry grasses. Most burrows have at least two entrances, and the temperature inside remains relatively warm in winter and cool in summer.

Top left: Members of a prairie dog neighborhood identify each other by "kissing" or nuzzling. Middle and bottom left: Prairie dogs take special care to maintain the burrow's entrance. They kick or push loose dirt onto the mound and then pack it tightly with their noses or foreheads; you can see the pattern of noseprints around many mounds.

Catching the first rays of the morning sun, a cautious prairie dog peeks over the edge of its burrow.

Burrowing owls never dig their own burrows. Here they have taken over an unused prairie dog home.

Prairie dogs and bison have coexisted on the prairie for thousands of years.

Hundreds of animal species live in or near prairie dog towns in the shortgrass and mixed-grass prairies.

It is hard to picture the prairie without seeing some animal grazing on it. Grazers such as bison and pronghorn antelope (which can cover ground at up to sixty-five miles per hour, twenty feet in a single leap!) are attracted to the grasses surrounding the mounds of prairie dog towns. Prairie dogs rejuvenate the soil with their digging and fertilize it with their droppings. Because they prune tall grasses, new growth is more abundant and nutritious for grazers.

Burrowing owls, small rodents, and rabbits are among those who make use of empty prairie dog burrows for their own shelter, especially when their young are born. Many insects also choose to inhabit prairie dog tunnels, and, of course, they draw insect-eating animals. A particularly common sight just inside the burrow opening is the poisonous black widow spider; the ominous sight of its red hourglass-shaped marking will make any person draw back from that mound in a hurry.

Perhaps the most frightening prairie inhabitant, however, is the rattlesnake. Rattlers don't need to wait until prairie dog burrows

Rattlesnakes are commonly seen on prairie dog towns.

are abandoned. When several crawl inside to hibernate in a slithery tangle, the prairie dogs plug up that section of tunnel and dig elsewhere.

It's an encounter with a rattlesnake that I consider one of my closest calls as a wildlife photographer. One day while driving through South Dakota, I spotted a rattlesnake stretched across the road and decided to pull off the road in my van and make sure the snake got safely across. To hurry along its rescue, I extended the legs of my tripod and poked at the long body. That snake's cold stare and black forked tongue almost got to me, but nearby was a very photogenic prickly pear cactus, and I could picture the snake next to it in my mind's eye—plant spines next to animal fangs.

So I picked up the snake with my tripod and deposited him near the cactus. I shot frame after frame, circling the snake to make him turn his head and aim that wonderfully scary tongue into the camera. I had a long lens on my camera and wasn't paying much attention to how close I was getting to the snake. Suddenly, he struck out at me, hitting my camera lens with his fangs and shooting venom all over it.

Naturally, I was scared at first, but since I knew I wasn't hurt, my concern focused on getting my expensive lens cleaned off. "Thanks, snake," I said before running back to my van. The lens wiped clean, I turned to the open side door of my van, ready to jump out. When I heard the *SSSSSST*, it was too late to stop my foot. The snake was coiled right below the step of my van; it seemed to be waiting for me, even though that would be very unsnakelike. I stepped virtually on top of him but was able to spring, unbitten, right back into my van. I sat inside for a long time, heart pounding . . . thinking. And, of course, I had a good look around before trying again to step down.

I still do this.

Facing page: Sharp teeth and sharp spines:
A rattlesnake is clearly unhappy about posing
for this portrait.

A formidable enemy of the prairie dog, the badger can completely excavate a burrow in minutes.

Champion digger with his prize.

The snake provided me with only one of many lessons I've learned about getting along with other animals during my years watching and photographing the prairie. Different species often co-exist and adapt to the presence of one another, and I witnessed a cooperative hunting strategy in a prairie dog town which was unique. Coyotes and badgers both eat prairie dogs, but a coyote can't dig very well. Badgers, on the other hand, have limbs that are designed for digging with strong muscles and long claws.

The badger starts at the entrance of the prairie dog burrow and forces its prey to escape through a secret opening. The coyote appears to anticipate this escape and watch for it, often grabbing the prairie dog as it exits. Who knows how many thousands of years of evolution taught the coyote to watch the badger invade a prairie dog burrow? Although it appears to be an unwilling participant, the badger often benefits. If the prairie dog manages to jump free of the coyote and back into the burrow, chances are good that it will be captured inside by the badger.

A young coyote pup seeks out the source of prairie dog chatter.

North America's rarest mammal, the black-footed ferret is shy and rarely seen.

Before venturing into the ferrets' dark cage, I had to take an antiseptic bath, replace my regular clothes with surgical gown and mask, and wipe down my camera equipment. I'll never forget that night shoot, feeling like an alien in that cage, occasionally catching a glimpse of eerie, emerald-green eyes.

Facing page: Prairie dogs have little control over wallowing bison.

Although many species have adapted to the unique ecosystem known as prairie dog towns, there is one animal that actually cannot exist in the wild without prairie dogs. The nocturnal black-footed ferret is the most endangered mammal in North America because of its close link to prairie dogs and their rapidly disappearing towns. The ferrets depend on prairie dogs as their primary source of food and shelter. Inside the burrows, black-footed ferrets sleep, escape harsh weather, store their food, hide from predators, and give birth to their young.

At one point there were only about eighteen black-footed ferrets left, so they have been bred in captivity for several years and carefully released into the wild. My only opportunity to photograph these rare creatures was at a breeding facility in Wyoming.

A unique connection exists, as well, between prairie dogs and bison. Bison are plagued by bloodthirsty insects, and they get rid of them by throwing dust or mud all over themselves. They drop to their knees, roll around, and kick with all four legs. This process, called wallowing, chokes the insects before they can bite.

The entrances to prairie dog burrows provide dirt pillows for the bison to lie upon.

Facing page: A midwinter hibernating prairie dog town in the Badlands National Park, South Dakota.

Unfortunately for the bison, the prairie is covered by dense grass and therefore is not an easy place to find loose piles of dirt for such "baths." So bison seek out prairie dog towns with the mounds of dirt that form their entrances and exits. Prairie dogs work endlessly, tamping down the soil with their noses and sculpting it to cone-shaped perfection—only to have a bison come along, drop to its knees, and roll around, instantly destroying the prairie dog's work. All the tiny creatures can do in retaliation is bark at the bison, wait patiently, and then rebuild. If their mounds are repeatedly flattened, the prairie dogs will give up and move.

As a natural, undisturbed ecosystem, prairie dog towns can last for centuries. But human needs often throw off the balance of nature. Ranchers blame prairie dogs for ruining the grasses needed by cattle, so they have been poisoning prairie dogs for years. But if prairie dogs and grazing animals don't mix, why do bison appear to thrive near prairie dog towns? It is too easy to concentrate on one creature that seems destructive and so abundant and forget that poisoning prairie dogs also reduces the numbers of all wildlife associated with the towns.

Billions of black-tailed prairie dogs used to occupy the prairies, their underground world stretching from Canada to Mexico. One town in Texas is known to have covered 25,000 square miles and sheltered more than 400 million prairie dogs. Today, their numbers nationwide have been reduced by more than 90 percent, and they live mainly on prairie land that is preserved and protected by the government. For centuries, these amiable rodents managed to survive the fiercest of fires and predators, the harshest extremes in hot and cold, wet and dry. None of their adaptive skills, however, prepared them for what was to come.

ᘛ ᘛ ᘛ *Chapter 4*

ONE PICTURE IS WORTH A THOUSAND WORDS

The positive reaction to my prairie dog photos in the Badlands book gave me the courage to approach *National Geographic*. At last, I had some of the credentials I needed to be treated seriously by this prestigious magazine's editors.

But it still took another three-week shoot in my home state of Minnesota—on my own and with no contract—to sell my work to the *Geographic*. Then, shortly after the editors bought two of my photos, I proposed to them a comprehensive story about the American prairie. The nature of this proposal—just my ideas, no pictures—shows how young and naive I was at the time. But I figured the prairie was, after all, a familiar landscape to me, and one that had nearly disappeared. It felt right and possible.

When I got word from the *Geographic* that they wanted to do my prairie story, it was one of the biggest moments in my life. I was alone, taking pictures in a remote part of the Texas prairie, when I got off the phone with one of the editors. Ready to explode with my news, I caught sight of a farmer in the distance, sitting on his tractor. I ran up to him, camera in hand, and said, "Hi, I'm from the *National Geographic*." He gave me this bemused, blank gaze. *The*

Facing page: Big bluestem prairie grass rises above its flowery neighbors in The Nature Conservancy's Ordway Prairie, South Dakota.

The golden arches on the edge of one of the last remnant tallgrass prairie patches near Chicago.

Facing page: The tallest of the tall grass at the peak of its season near the shores of Lake Michigan in Wisconsin.

what? He'd never heard of it. I often recall this lesson in humility when I need to be brought back down to earth.

One of the reasons the *Geographic* accepted my proposal was that environmental groups had started, during the 1970s, to push for restoration of the American prairie. The *Geographic* story, published in January 1980, was entitled "The Tallgrass Prairie: Can It Be Saved?" Written by Kansas-raised Dennis Farney, the article sounded warnings about the demise of the tallgrass prairie, especially in Illinois, the so-called Prairie State. At present, barely 3,500 acres remain of the thirty-seven million acres of former tallgrass prairie in Illinois.

The 1980 *Geographic* article profiled a handful of people on both sides: ranchers and farmers who resisted prairie revival and preservationists whose activities ranged from the expansion of national

A whitetail deer fawn is dwarfed by big bluestem at Blue Mounds State Park, Minnesota.

parks and prairie preserves to the painstaking collection of wild-flower seeds to plant in backyard gardens. I was somewhat disappointed that the photos the *Geographic* chose focused more on people than on nature. Still, the story represents an important beginning for my career and a crucial change in public awareness.

Although pictures are never enough, wildlife photography is a kind of environmental activism. It reminds people what we have on this planet and what we are in danger of losing. It's gratifying for me to know that my work has helped to raise awareness of the American prairie—both of its graceful splendor and of its systematic destruction.

Chapter 5

SOME BUFFALO
STILL ROAM

Almost twenty years after my first *Geographic* assignment, I found myself once again returning to the prairie for another *Geographic* article. And this time I knew for certain that nature would be my focus. It's particularly poignant for me to look at those photos taken for the article in my own "backyard"—the Blue Mounds. During the years since my childhood, 1,500 acres of land near my home were set aside as the Blue Mounds State Park. My *Geographic* photo of a bison against a sunset was taken in almost the exact same spot as the one I took of the fox when I was a boy.

It's not surprising that one of the earliest and most significant efforts toward prairie revival was the return of the bison. What animal better symbolizes the power and majesty of this natural landscape?

Plains Indians coexisted very effectively with bison for thousands of years in North America. Indians made use of nearly every part of the bison, including its blood and bones. But they never made much of a dent in the bison population.

When pioneers headed west to settle in the wilderness, bison

A symbolic sunset with a cow buffalo.
Bison herds once numbered in the millions.

33

The bison herd used for the movie Dances with Wolves *occupies a place called Houck Ranch in South Dakota. Privately owned, it boasts 100 square miles of land and about 4,000 American bison. This ranch has provided me with many of my photographs of bison over the years.*

provided them with food and clothing. In addition, hunting and killing the bison became a popular pioneer sport. One form of "entertainment" offered by the railroads in the West was the opportunity to shoot animals from moving trains. The senseless slaughter left hundreds of bison, antelope, and wolf carcasses to rot along the tracks. This practice left the Indians of the area baffled and grief-stricken—and often starving as well.

As the number of settlers increased and their habitat was turned into farms and ranches, the bison population dropped from perhaps as many as sixty million down to about 500. Conservation efforts since the early 1900s, however, have saved the bison from extinction.

Bison now number in the hundreds of thousands. They are grazing on Indian reservations, on private preserves, and on more than 1,000 ranches. And they are not just tourist attractions. Some ranchers are hoping that Americans will begin choosing bison meat over beef. Changes in our eating habits take time, of course. Most of us are not yet eating "buffalo-burgers," but it's important to note that bison meat is much leaner and healthier than beef. And it's actually quite delicious.

Bison graze more efficiently and are better able than cattle to survive the extremes in weather on the prairie, even drought and blizzards. Bison herds are, unfortunately, more difficult to contain than cattle. Such a radical change on the part of ranchers will take time and patience.

Most people think of a bison as a kind of big shaggy cow, and some even approach them in national parks to put their children on those broad, inviting backs. Big mistake. Many severe injuries and deaths occur because of the underrated danger of bison. During a recent visit to Yellowstone, I learned of a man who had just been disemboweled by the curved horn of a bison. And once, while

Prairie coneflowers in the path of a grazing bison.

Bison calf nurses under the watchful eye of its mother.

photographing a herd, I suddenly found myself charged by a female bison protecting her calf. I barely made it back to my van intact.

Bison reach an adult height of over six feet tall, making them the largest North American land mammal. A male bison weighs up to 2,000 pounds; a female, more than 1,000 pounds. Both male and female bison have horns that are never shed and can grow up to twenty-six inches long. The horn is often used to pick up an attacker and toss it so high that the fall alone can kill it.

Saving the bison was only part of the problem facing conservationists. During the 1970s, they tried to protect parts of the remaining grasslands, but they were opposed, naturally, by the farmers and ranchers who feared losing their land and livelihood to natural parks and preserves. It wasn't until scores of farms failed during the 1980s that people began to look more closely at what we had done to the prairie in the last 100 years. Not only were the grasslands destroyed, but the land itself had become used up.

After years of planting the same crops in the same fields and grazing and mowing the same pastures over and over, we had robbed the soil of its natural nutrients. Chemical fertilizers, herbicides, and insecticides became necessary for crops to survive, and these polluted the water. Towns surrounded by and supported by farms began to empty as family farms disappeared.

Now things are changing. It appears that more and more people are learning to imitate nature rather than trying to control it. They are experimenting with new ways of raising cattle, bringing back native grasses for grazing in order to restore and preserve the soil.

One of the finest remnants of the tallgrass prairie is the Tallgrass Prairie Preserve in Oklahoma.

Or they divide pastures so that cows feed for a few days in one area, then move elsewhere so the prairie can recover.

Other hopeful signs can be seen in the preserves appearing across the plains states. One of the best examples is the Tallgrass Prairie Preserve in Oklahoma, one of several owned and managed by The Nature Conservancy; here you can lose yourself in fifty square miles of grass and wildflowers and sky. On many of its preserves, the Conservancy uses controlled fires and grazing to bring the landscape back to its natural balance. Bison are a big part of these preserves, both for grazing and for attracting the visitors who help finance these efforts.

The Nature Conservancy is a private organization with 650,000 members, but government agencies are becoming more involved as well; state and federal funding will play an important role in the future. Our elected officials need to know that we feel an urgency about this issue, and that something can, in fact, be done.

A wild prairie rose in the midst of not-so-wild bluegrass.

My attachment to the American prairie comes not only from my childhood but from a lifetime of exploration and photography. I still dream of seeing the fragments of preserved prairie grow ever larger until many of them connect. Then it may be possible, once again, to look across the horizon at unbroken grassland, bursting with the color and wild energy of the American prairie.

Facing page: A small group of bison framed by black-eyed Susan.

EPILOGUE

The lure of prairie grass. A place known as the Blue Mounds and the enchantment of all that used to lie behind the hills. A young red fox. A three-dollar camera. Not, perhaps, the most promising start for a career. But something more had led me to pursue that fox with my camera. It was a book.

I found myself in the Luverne school library one day when I was in the seventh or eighth grade. This was not a common place for me to be since I was not a good student and had not yet found books to be nearly as exciting as what awaited me outdoors.

From one of the shelves, I pulled a book. I wish now that I could remember the title. It was the story of a young wildlife photographer. The book contained no photos, strictly words. But I took it home and, for the first time in my life, got lost in a story. Those words painted an exquisite picture of one boy and the world seen through the lens of his camera. I read those words and suddenly said "yes." I didn't immediately vow to go out and take wildlife pictures, but something was awakened in me.

This is the way of all beginnings, I think. Paying attention to the fragile connections between experiences and listening to the voices within us. And the world can open up to us in ways we could never have imagined.

Hungry horned lark chicks mimic the blossoms of the first blooming pasqueflower on the North Dakota prairie.

ꙮ ꙮ ꙮ *Appendix: Get Involved*

To contact The Nature Conservancy, you may find local chapters listed in the white pages of your phone book, or write to:

The Nature Conservancy Headquarters
1815 North Lynn Street
Arlington, VA 22209
(800) 628-6860 and (703) 841-5300

If you wish to get more information about specific prairie preserves, write to:

Blue Mounds State Park
Route 1, Box 52
Luverne, MN 56156
(507) 283-4892

Niobrara Preserve
Route 1, Box 348
Johnstown, NE 69214
(402) 722-4440

Tallgrass Prairie Preserve
P. O. Box 458
Pawhuska, OK 74056
(918) 287-4803

Cross Ranch
HC 2, Box 150
Hensler, ND 58530
(701) 794-8741

Ordway Preserve
Star Route 1, Box 16
Leola, SD 57456
(605) 439-3475

Western Preserve Office
Route 2, Box 240
Glyndon, MN 56547
(218) 498-2679

ꙮ ꙮ ꙮ *Index*